Designer: Shawn Dahl, dahlimama inc

ISBN 978-1-4197-1578-5

Copyright © 2015 Abrams Noterie

Printed in China

Abrams Noterie products are available at special discounts
when purchased in quantity for premiums and promotions
as well as fundraising or educational use. Special editions
can also be created to specification. For details, contact
specialsales@abramsbooks.com or the address below.

THE ART OF BOOKS SINCE 1949
115 West 18th Street
New York, NY 10011
www.abramsbooks.com